CONTENTS

INTRODUCTION

Welcome to *Rock Guitar Fundamentals*! Here you will learn the foundational skills you need to play rock guitar.

This guide is divided into three main parts: reading tablature, rhythm guitar basics, and lead guitar basics. Each section gives you what you need in order to start learning how to play rock in all its genres with more confidence. Once you understand these basics, you'll be able to start playing tons of great songs!

So let's get started.

TABLATURE

Tablature (or TAB) is the most popular way of learning new songs on the guitar. It is almost as old as standard notation for stringed instruments. TAB is easy to read and allows you to figure out songs much faster than standard notation. However, there are some drawbacks. Most TABS do not include any rhythm, meaning you have to either know how the song is supposed to sound ahead of time or rely on the standard notation, when available.

Tablature shows you *where* to play, while standard notation shows you *what* to play. Therefore, both are equally valuable when learning a new song. (Note: Standard notation is not covered in this guide, but is a useful skill to develop in the future.)

To read tablature, start with the bottom line. This line represents the thickest string on your guitar. Each successive line is a new string. Therefore the top line is the highest string. (See Chart Below). The numbers placed on these lines indicate a fret number. A zero means an open string, or no fingers. For example, if there is a 5 on the bottom line, that means you are to play the fifth fret on the last string. If there is a zero on the second line from the bottom, you'll play the fifth string open.

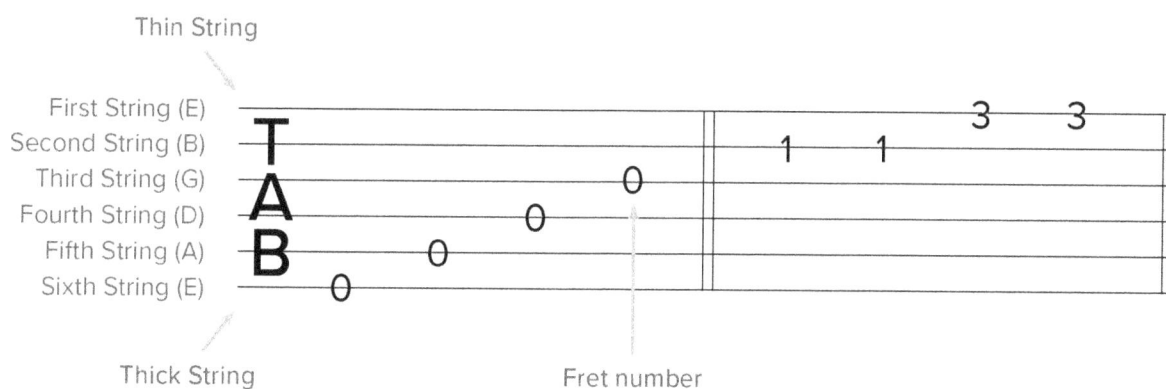

The fret numbers indicate where to place your fingers.

TAB PRACTICE: ONE NOTE AT A TIME

In Exercise 1 below, you will see tablature divided into sections called **measures** or **bars** using vertical bar lines. This is done to make it easier to read and to imply a grouping of beats, much like you'd see in standard musical notation. The tablature diagram on the previous page uses a double bar line. This can be seen in both examples below, where the ending bar line is thicker, indicating the end of the exercise or example.

Try it: Practice reading and playing tablature with the exercises below.

Exercise 1: Notes on the first and second strings.

```
T --0---0---1---1----3---3---5---5---|---------------------------|-----------------||
A -------------------------------------0---0---1---1----3---3---1---|
B
```

Exercise 2: Notes on the fifth and sixth strings.

```
T -------------------------|-------------------|---------------------||
A -------------------------|-------------------|---------------------||
B --0---0---1---1----0---0---2---3---|--0---0---1---1----0---0---2---3---||
```

Exercise 3: See if you can guess the name of this "happy" tune.

```
T ------------------1---|--0-----------------|------------3---1--------0---0--
A --0---0---2---0-------|--------0---0---2----|--0---------------------------
B
```

```
-3-------0--------------|-----------------1---1---0--|--------------1----------||
--------------1-----0---|--------2---------------------|--1---3---1------------||
```

Exercise 4

```
T
A
B   0   0   3   3 | 2   2   0   0 |   0   0   3   3 | 2   2   0   0 |
```

Exercise 5

```
T
A
B  0   0   3   0 | 0   0   3   3   0 |   0   0   3   0 |
                                                   3   3   0   3       0
```

```
                                              2   2   0   0
  0     0   3   0 |  0   0   3   3   0 |             2   2   0 |
                                                           3       0
```

Exercise 6

```
T
A
B   0   0   3   4   2   2   4   2 | 0   0   3   4   2   2   4   2 |   0   0   3   4   2   2   4   2 | 0   0   3   4   2   2   4   2 |
```

```
  2   2   2   2   2   2   2   2 | 0   0   0   0   0   0   0   0 |                    2   2   4   2 |                    2   2   4   2 |
                                                           0   0   3   4         0   0   3   4
```

4

PLAYING MORE THAN ONE NOTE AT THE SAME TIME

There will be many instances where songs will include more than just the melody, meaning that you will have to read more than one note at the same time. To do this, simply play only the strings indicated in the tablature. (See below.)

Exercise 1: Only play the strings with numbers on them. For measure 1, you'll play the thickest string open and the note found on the fifth string second fret at the same time.

Exercise 2: Read the tab carefully and take your time.

Exercise 3: A Fun Riff.

Exercise 4: Classic Rock Riff

Try Out These Recognizable Riffs

United Front

```
T|------------0---------|----------------------|------------0---------|----------------------|
A|--2-----2-------2-----|--0---------------2---|--2-----2-------2-----|--0-------------------|
B|----------------------|--------3-----2-------|----------------------|--------3-----2-------|
```

Be Yourself

```
----------------------|--0-------0-----------|----------------2-----|------------2---------|
--0---0---1---2-------|--------2-------2--2--1---0----------0---0----|----------------------|
```

Fire Water

```
--0-----3-----5-------|--0-----3-----6-----5-|--0-----3-----5-----3-|--0-------------------|
--0-----3-----5-------|--0-----3-----6-----5-|--0-----3-----5-----3-|--0-------------------|
```

Full Grit

```
--5---------5---3---5-|------5---3---5-------|------5---------------|
--3---------3---1---3-|------3---1---3-------|------3---5---6-------|
--------------------------------------------------------3---4-----|
```

Metal One

```
------4-------0-------|------4-------0-------|------4-------0-------|------4-------0-----0-|
--2-------2-----------|------------------3---|--2-------2----------|------------3---3-----|
--------------3-----3-|                      |                     |
```

```
------4-------0-------|------4-------0-------|------4-------0-------|----------------------|
--2-------2-----------|--------------0---0---|                     |------------2-----2---|
                      |                      |------3-------3------|--0-------2----------|
```

RHYTHM

Rhythm is essentially the idea of how long or how short you hold a chord or note. In this book, and in many other guitar publications, you will find guitar chords written as a chord symbol with slash-notation to show you how each chord is to be played. (See "Basic Rhythms" below).

It should be noted that plenty of publications, including most fake books, leave the strum pattern entirely up to you. Therefore, it is helpful to have several strum patterns learned and at your disposal.

Below you will find the most common rhythms used by rhythm guitar players.

Basic Rhythms

	Whole Note Rhythm Slash				Half Note Rhythm Slash				Quarter Note Rhythm Slash			
Count:	1	(2	3	4)	1	(2)	3	(4)	1	2	3	4
Strum:	Strum	Hold	Hold	Hold	Strum	Hold	Strum	Hold	Strum	Strum	Strum	Strum

Divided Rhythms

Eighth Note Rhythm Slash   Sixteenth Note Rhythm Slash

1 & 2 & 3 & 4 &   1 e & a 2 e & a 3 e & a 4 e & a

Sixteenth Note Variation Rhythms

1 &a 2 &a 3 &a 4 &a   1e & 2e & 3e & 4 e&   1 e a 2e a 3e a 4e a

Dotted Rhythms

1 (2 3) Rest   1 (& 2) & 3 (& 4) &   1 a 2 a 3 a 4 a

Rests

Whole Note Rest   Half Note Rest   Quarter Note Rests   Eighth Note Rests   Sixteenth Note Rests

6/8 Time

Count: 1 (2 3) 4 (5 6)   1 2 3   4 5 6   1 & 2 & 3 &   4 & 5 & 6 &

8

POWER CHORDS

Power chords, also known as "rock chords", are two to three note chords whose tonalities are neither major nor minor. A major chord, for example, contains three main notes: a root, a major third, and a fifth. The chord C major is made up of the root C, the major third E, and the fifth G. The chord C minor contains the notes C, the minor third Eb, and the fifth G. So as you can see, it is the third of the chord that determines whether or not chord has a major or minor sound.

A power chord only contains two of these notes: the root and the fifth (meaning of course, a note five notes away from the root).

Example: C   D   E   F   G

1   2   3   4   5

Therefore, the chord symbol representing the power chord will be shown like this: C5. This means that the chord is a C chord, but the only other note included is the fifth of the chord, so in this case, G.

One of the nice things about learning power chords is that they are moveable shapes. This means that you learn where to place your fingers to get the chord, but then you can move that shape all over the neck and achieve the same sound at different pitch levels. In other words, you are learning one chord that can be moved up and down the strings. So instead of focusing on where to place your fingers, your focus is on which fret will produce the right chord. As a result, learning power chords helps you learn your neck faster.

Since they are only made up of two primary notes, and since those notes are fairly far apart, they are perfect for adding effects to, like distortion. If you add distortion to a regular major or minor chord, the result is often a muddy, indistinct sound. However, the power chord does not have this issue. In fact, effects often help the chord to sound fuller.

On the next page, you'll start with open voiced power chords, meaning that one of the two notes is played on an open string. E5, for example, is played by pressing down at fret 2 on string 5, and then striking the open 6th string along with the fretted note at the same time. With the A5 power chord, make sure you don't play the thickest string. And with the D5 only play strings 4 and 3.

OPEN POWER CHORDS

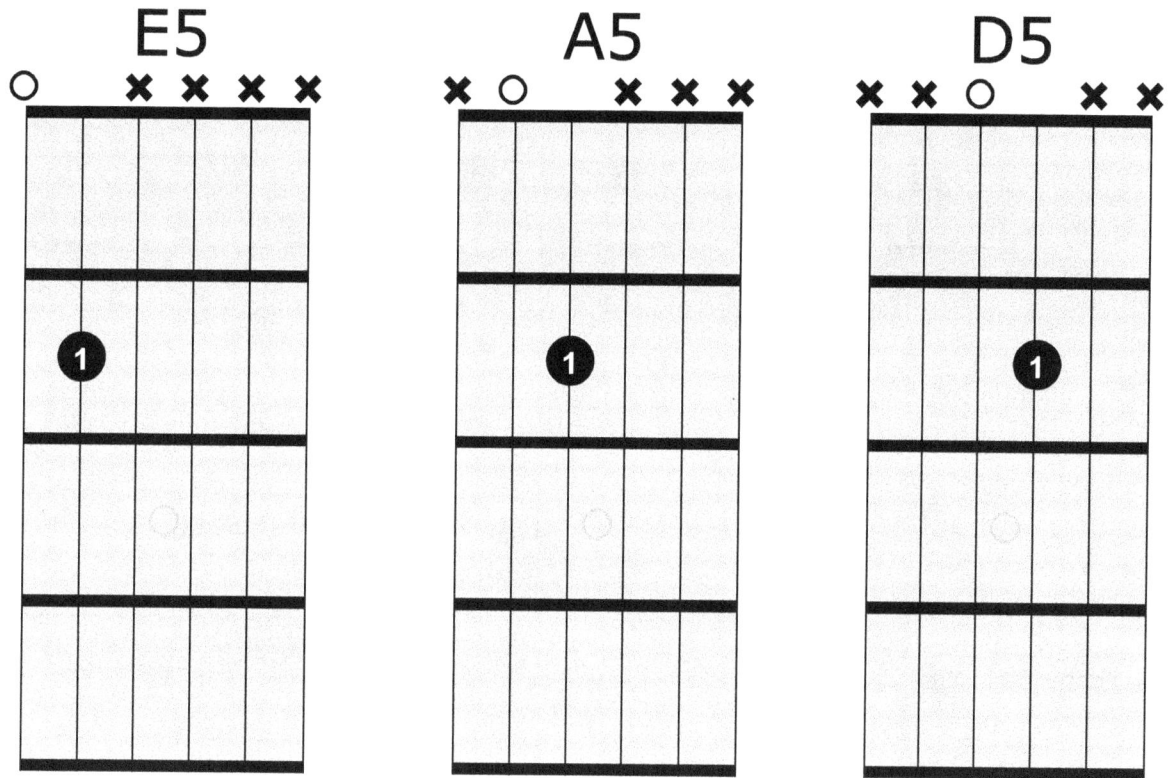

Try it: Practice strumming the two-note, open power chords below. Be sure to only strum the two strings indicated in the above charts.

Never read a chord diagram before? Check out the guide in the appendix (page 35).

Practicing Open Power Chords

Exercise 1

Exercise 2

Exercise 3

Exercise 4

D5   **A5**

D5   **A5**

Exercise 5

A5

D5   **A5**

E5   **A5**

ROOT 6 POWER CHORDS

Since power chords only consist of two notes, it becomes possible to play these chords easily all over the neck.

To begin, take the E5 power chord. Then move the note on the second fret up by a half step to fret 3. Next, place your index finger on the first fret of the last string. This chord shape is the F5 power chord. This shape can be moved up the string. As you move, each new position on the neck becomes a new power chord.

The chart below shows you the natural notes on the sixth string, which are the root notes of the power chords. Therefore, if you take the F5 shape (shown below) and move it up to the third fret, the resulting chord is a G5 power chord. Since the root (or primary sound) of the chord is located on string six, it is called a root 6 power chord.

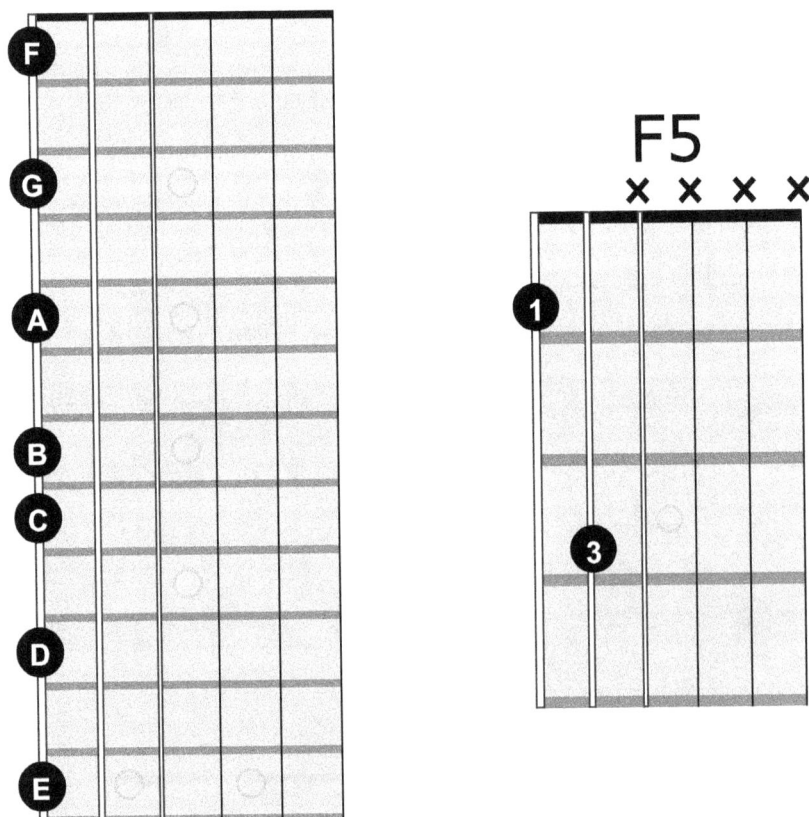

F5

Try it: Practice strumming the two-note, root 6 power chords below. Be sure to only strum the two strings indicated in the chart on the previous page.

Open
E5

First Fret
F5

E5

Third Fret
G5

E5

Practicing Root 6 Power Chords

Exercise 1

G5   F5   G5   F5   E5

Exercise 2

A5   G5   A5   F5   G5

Exercise 3

B5 — C5 — B5 — C5 — G5 — A5 — B5 — C5

Exercise 4

D5 — A5 — D5

Exercise 5

E5 — D5 — C5 — E5

Exercise 6

E5 — D5 — C5 — B5 — A5 — G5 — F5 — E5

15

Exercise 7

G5   C5   D5   G5

Exercise 8

C5   A5   C5   A5   F5   G5   C5

Exercise 9

A5   B5   C5   B5   A5   B5   C5   B5

D5   E5   A5   B5   A5

ROOT 5 POWER CHORDS

Root 5 power chords work in the same manner as the root 6. However, with this set of chords, since the root of the chord is on the fifth string, the sixth string is not played. Also note that the first natural note on this string is the B natural, found on the second fret of the fifth string.

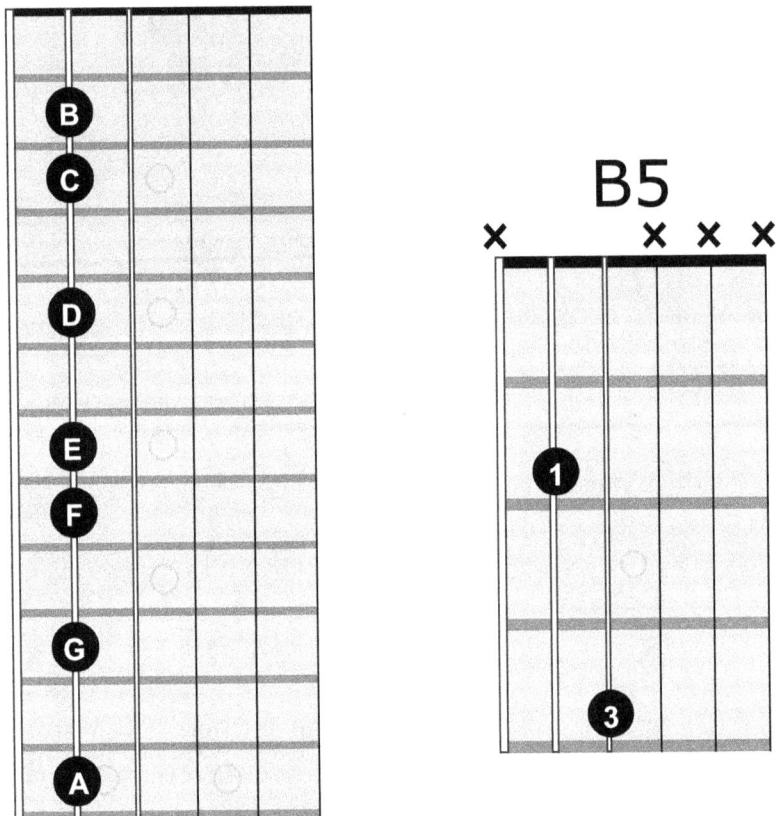

Practicing Root 5 Power Chords

Exercise 1

Exercise 2

D5 **C5** **E5** **D5**

Exercise 3

E5 **F5** **E5** **F5** **E5**

Exercise 4

G5 **A5** **F5** **E5** **G5** **A5**

Exercise 5

A5 **G5** **F5** **E5** **D5** **C5** **B5** **A5**

Exercise 6

Exercise 7

Exercise 8

Exercise 9

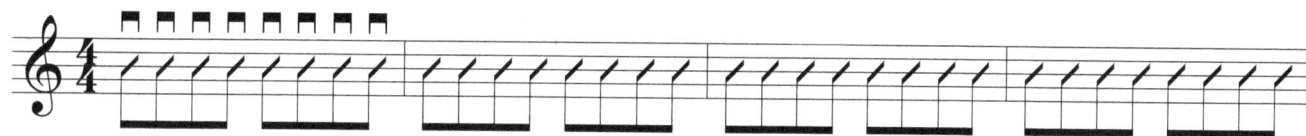

ROOT 5 & ROOT 6 COMBINED

In this lesson, will we be practicing playing power chords in a more practical manner by switching between strings rather than staying on one string like we have in the two previous lessons. This is by far the more common way of playing power chords.

Since there are now so many options for playing the same thing, a general rule you'll want to follow is this: ask yourself what version of the chord is closest to where you are now? Then move to that chord.

For example, if you were to play a root 6 G5 chord and wanted to play C5 power chord next, you would simply move from the G5 on the last string third fret to the fifth string third fret C5 power chord rather than skipping all the way up to the eighth fret on the sixth string.

Exercise 1

Exercise 2

Exercise 3

Exercise 4

Exercise 5

LEAD GUITAR

The E Minor Pentatonic Scale

Now that you have learned a bit of rhythm guitar, we'll move on to lead guitar, which of course means understanding how to craft a guitar solo. We'll begin with the pentatonic scale, which is a five-note scale (as opposed to the more traditional seven-note major and minor scales) that is used in all sorts of music, but is associated most closely with rock guitar. (In fact, I know several teachers who call it the "rock-ta-tonic" scale).

Let's begin with the basic five notes that make up the scale. For this book, all examples are in the key of E minor. Therefore, the five notes in this scale are E G A B D. Try them out in open position in the exercise below.

Exercise 1: The E Minor Pentatonic Scale in one octave

Next, we'll expand this idea so that every E G A B and D are played in one region of the neck, starting with the last string open and moving to the first string, third fret. (Shown both in the chart below and in Exercise 2 on the next page.)

Exercise 2: The E Minor Pentatonic Scale in one region of the fretboard

Exercise 3: Now play the E Minor Pentatonic scale using eighth notes for a more fluid sound.

⊓ = Pick Down

V = Pick Up

USING THE PENTATONIC SCALE TO START SOLOING

Now we are going to take the pentatonic scale and play it with three different sets of chord. Each set will give the scale a different sound. The first set of chords is a 12-bar blues form using major chords. This clash of major chords with a minor scale is what gives the blues and rock its distinctive sound. The second set of chords are a minor 12-bar blues. The third set uses power chords, which are not major or minor, giving it an even more rock feel.

Note: The double dot found in the next to last measure is a repeat sign, so you would play the song again before playing the final note.

To practice these exercises, either record yourself playing these chords and jam along, or look for the 12-bar blues backing tracks found on my YouTube Channel: The Missing Method for Guitar.

Exercise 4: 12-Bar Blues in E

Get the 12-bar blues backing tracks here: https://bit.ly/12-bar-blues.

Exercise 5: 12-Bar Blues in E Minor

Em

```
T |----------------------------------|------------------------|----0--3------3--0----|--3--0------------------|
A |--------0--2-----------------------|--0--2------0--2--------|----------------------|----------3--0----------|
B |--0--3-----------------------------|------------------------|----------------------|------------------------|
```

Am   Em

```
T |----------------------------------|------------------------|----0--3------3--0----|--3--0------------------|
A |--------0--2-----------------------|--0--2------0--2--------|----------------------|----------3--0----------|
B |--0--3-----------------------------|------------------------|----------------------|------------------------|
```

B7   Am   Em   B7   Em

```
T |----------------------------------|------------------------|----------------------|--------0--2---.-----------|
A |--0--2------0--2----0--2------0--2-|------------0--2--------|--0--2------0--2---.------|-----0--|
B |------------------------0--3-------|------------------------|----------------------|--------------------0------|
```

Exercise 6: 12-Bar Blues with Power Chords

E5

```
T |----------------------------------|------------------------|----0--3------3--0----|----------------------|
A |--------0--2-----------------------|--0--2------0--2--------|----------------------|----------3--0--------|
B |--0--3-----------------------------|------------------------|----------------------|------------------------|
```

A5   E5

```
T |----------------------------------|------------------------|----0--3------3--0----|----------------------|
A |--------0--2-----------------------|--0--2------0--2--------|----------------------|----------3--0--------|
B |--0--3-----------------------------|------------------------|----------------------|------------------------|
```

B5   A5   E5   B5   E5

```
T |----------------------------------|------------------------|----------------------|--------0--2---.-----------|
A |--0--2------0--2----0--2------0--2-|------------0--2--------|--0--2------0--2---.------|-----0--|
B |------------------------0--3-------|------------------------|----------------------|--------------------0------|
```

Improvising a Solo

Now that you can play this scale along with these chords, let's take the next step and improvise a solo. Again, the 12-bar blues will be our reference point. To begin, simply take one note and play over these chords.

Once you've done that, use two notes. Then add one or more notes until you are able to comfortably play every note of the pentatonic scale. Do keep in mind that you don't have to play every note in every solo. You can use as many or as few notes as you think sounds good.

Example One-Note Solo

Tips for Developing a Solo

1. Keep it simple.

2. Use contrasting ideas

   For example, if you use a few notes for a measure or two, use more notes for the next two measures. Or if your first melody moves upward, have your next set of notes move downward, etc.

3. Find the root note of each chord and emphasize it. (Example: on an E chord, use the E note as your focal point.)

4. Use a variety of rhythms to add interest and contrast.

5. Reuse ideas to create a sense of unity. (In musical terms this is called "developing a motif.")

12-Bar Blues for Soloing:

Get the 12-bar blues backing tracks here: https://bit.ly/12-bar-blues.

To play this, go to the 12-bar blues backing tracks playlist on YouTube, and play along. Start with the slowest version (69 BPM) and work up to 108 BPM.

ARTICULATION

Articulation refers to any technique that adds an expressive element to your playing. It's basically using your hands to add sound effects that only a guitar (or similar stringed instrument) can do. Below you will find some of the most commonly used rock guitar techniques.

Half-Step Bend: Play the note, then bend the string a half-step so that it sounds like the next fret.

Whole-Step Bend: Play the note, then bend the string a whole-step.

Quarter-Step Bend: Play the note, then bend the string a quarter-step.

Grace Note Bend: Play the note, then bend the string right away as indicated.

Bend and Release: Play the note, bend the string as indicated, then return to the original note.

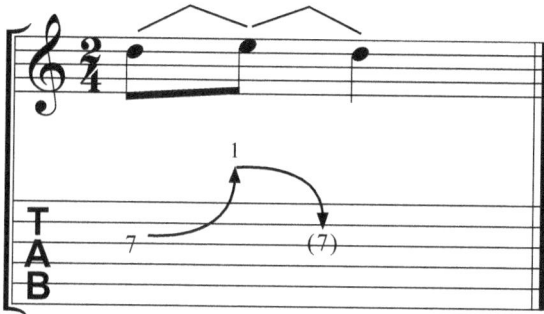

Pre-Bend: Bend to the desired pitch, then play the note.

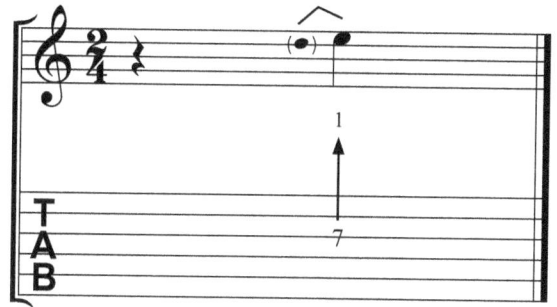

Hammer On: Play the first note with the first finger, then without picking, hammer down the third finger onto the second note so that it sounds.

Pull Off: (Also called a **Pluck-Off**) Place both fingers down first, one on the D, one on the C, then using the finger on the note D, pull the finger off so that the note below it is heard.

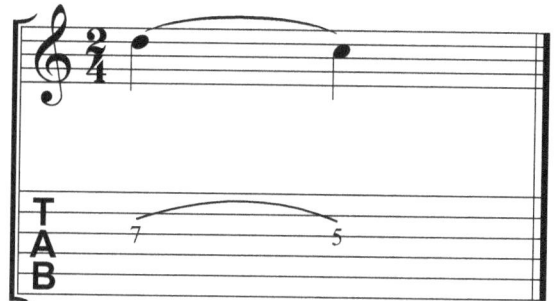

Slides: Play the first note, then without lifting your finger off, slide to the next note. (The example below is a descending slide. They can also go the other direction.)

Vibrato: Bend and release the note rapidly creating a "wave-like" sound effect.

ROCK GUITAR TONE

Now that you can play some of the foundational elements of rock guitar, another basic element you'll want to consider is tone. **Tone** simply refers to the sounds you are getting from your instrument. This is achieved by a variety of factors including: the type of strings you are using, the amp, effects, and the types of pick-ups. Different woods can also make a difference, but with electric guitars it's the pick-ups that really affect the sound.

One of the primary sounds you'll want to use is an effect called **distortion**. There are three main types of distortion: overdrive, fuzz, and full distortion. Each one is used for different styles of rock guitar. Classic rock, for example, uses a lot of overdrive. Fuzz is found in music by a great deal of alternative rock bands, and full distortion is used by hard rock and metal bands. These are of course generalities, with plenty of exceptions.

To get a basic distortion sound, make sure your guitar's volume is at 8 or 9 (you don't want to go all the way up just yet. It's always a good idea to give yourself a little room for extra volume when you need it.) Next, set the amp volume to 1. Then turn up the gain (or *presence*--this depends on the type of amp you have) to 8-10. If your amp has treble, midrange, and bass, turn those to either 5 or 7 to get a flat baseline to work from later on. Then slowly turn up your volume until you get a distortion sound.

Some amps have a separate distortion channel. In that case, make sure you engage that channel before trying it out. If you find you having trouble getting the sound you want from your amp, try a distortion pedal. I'd recommend the Boss DS-1. It's relatively inexpensive and works great on most amps. It's also been used on countless recordings.

Besides distortion, there are many other added effects that you can employ to get cool tones from your instrument. These include time-based effects, such as reverb and delay; modulation effects like flanger and chorus; and volume effects like wah-wah. There are many others, but these are the basic sounds many guitar players like to use. What I'd recommend is to buy an inexpensive multi-effects processor. That way you can play around with all these different sounds to see what you like or use most frequently. Once you know, then you can start acquiring the individual pedals dedicated to these sounds. However, for most players a multi-effects processor will do the job just fine.

NEXT STEPS

Congratulations! You now know the fundamental elements you need to play rock music on guitar! Of course, you'll want continue to practice what you just learned until each exercise is easy to play.

Among the skills we've touched on here, you've learned how to play the pentatonic scale in the open position. Once you have this down, you'll want to move on to the second position, and then learn the scale over the entire fretboard.

To do this easily, we created *Pentatonic Master*. This book will take you through each position, step-by-step so you can master this vital scale. The exercises you will find there work great as warm-ups so they are easy to incorporate into any practice session.

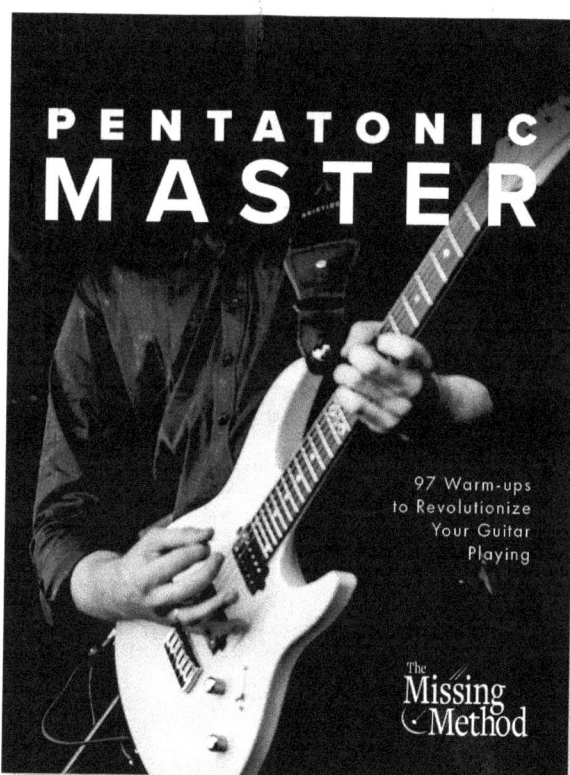

Find it & more at TheMissingMethod.com.

Want More Power Chord Practice?

Guitar Chord Master 3: Power Chords is a big book (185 pages) containing everything you need to master power chords. It reviews and builds on what you've already learned, and gives you even more practice. It will also teach you inverted power chords, and it has a special section on drop D tuning power chords.

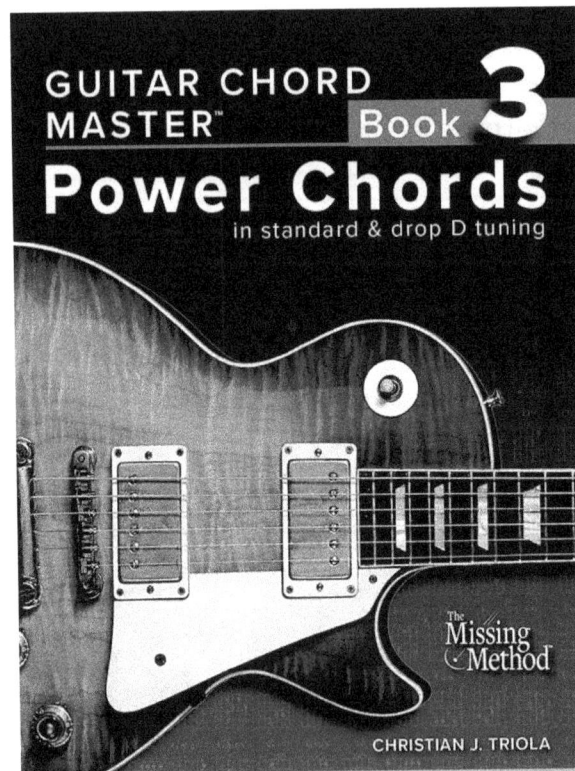

Find it & more at TheMissingMethod.com.

HOW TO READ A FRETBOARD DIAGRAM

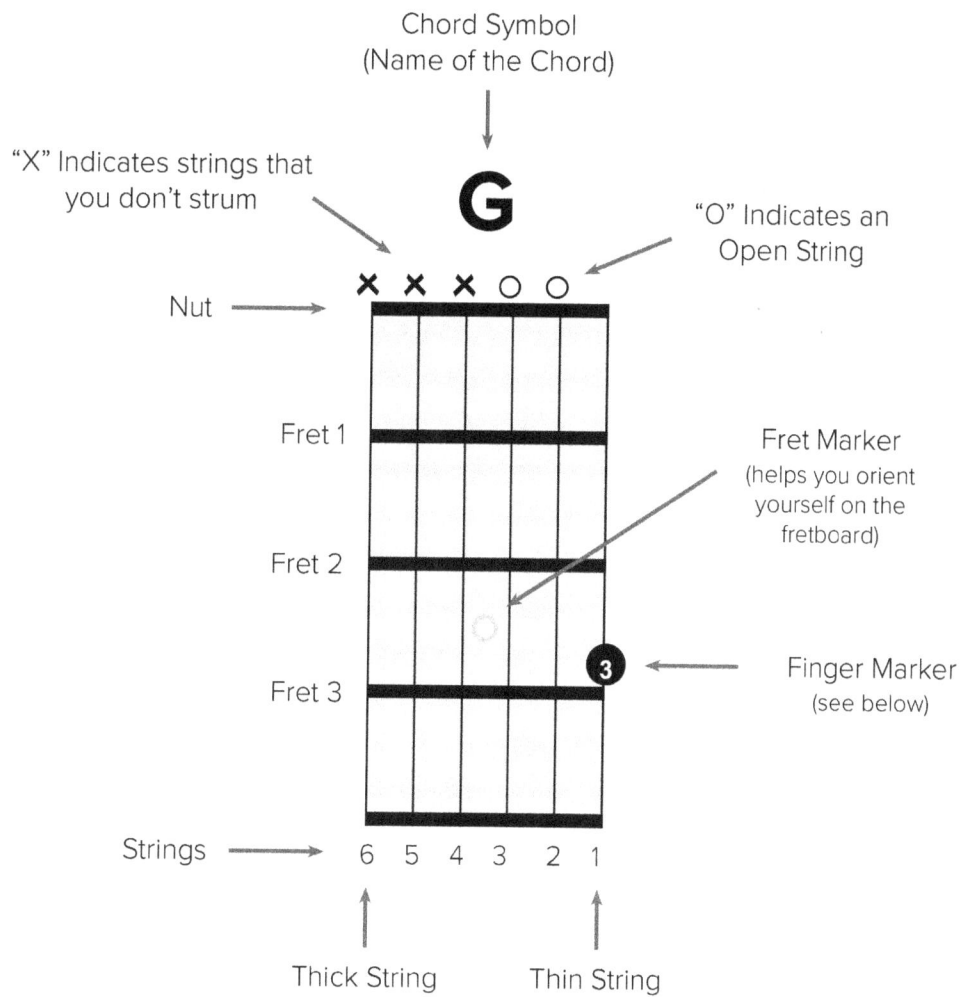

Chord Symbol
(Name of the Chord)

G

"X" Indicates strings that
you don't strum

"O" Indicates an
Open String

Nut ⟶

× × × O O

Fret 1

Fret Marker
(helps you orient
yourself on the
fretboard)

Fret 2

Fret 3

3

Finger Marker
(see below)

Strings ⟶ 6 5 4 3 2 1

Thick String   Thin String

2
1   3
    4

The finger markers correspond to the
fingers as numbered to the right ⟶

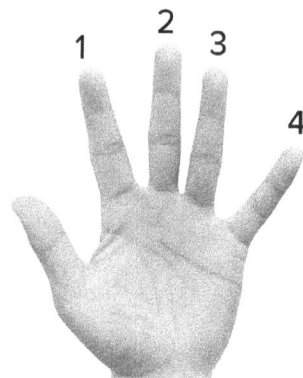

Technique Tip:

When placing fingers on the fretboard, always keep your wrist dropped and your fingers on their tips. Remember: only your fingertips and the thumb behind the neck should be touching the guitar. Keep the palm of your hand off the neck. This will help you build finger strength and solid technique.

HOW TO TUNE YOUR GUITAR

(1) The first thing you need to know in order to tune your guitar is what notes to tune to. In music, every different sound is given a name. The pitches are given letter names to make them easy to refer to. They are: A B C D E F G. On the guitar, each string is tuned to a specific pitch so that everything sounds the way it's supposed to. The chart below shows you the pitches of each string.

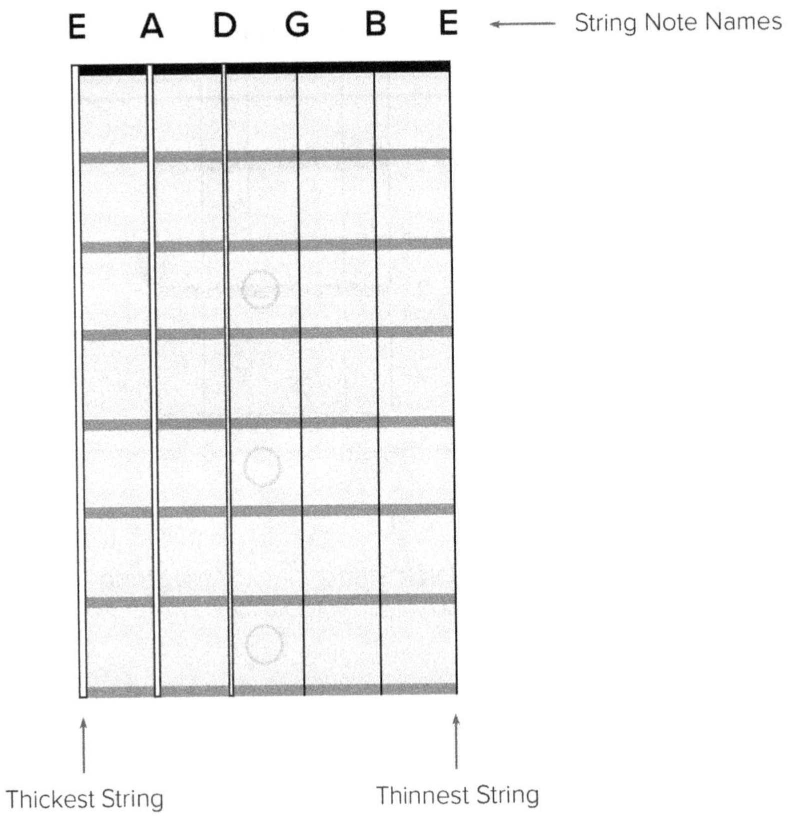

E	A	D	G	B	E

← String Note Names

↑ Thickest String   ↑ Thinnest String

There are a couple of sayings that can help you remember the names of the strings, from thick to thin:

Eddie **A**te **D**ynamite, **G**ood **B**ye **E**ddie.

Or the less violent:

Every **A**mateur **D**oes **G**et **B**etter **E**ventually.

(2) The second thing you should know is that tuning takes practice. It can be a little frustrating at first, but once you've done it a few times it gets easier and easier.

(3) The third thing you need to know is that most of the time your guitar will only need slight adjustments. Once it's in tune, it will usually stay fairly close to tune most of the time. However, it is recommended that you check your tuning every time you pick up the guitar. Be sure to listen carefully to the sound of an in-tune guitar, so you become familiar with what it should sound like.

(4) Now that you know this, we can begin tuning the guitar. There are several tuning methods. The best method is to buy a guitar tuner and learn how to use it.

Typically, most tuners will show which note you are playing and then tell you whether or not the note is too low, too high, or in tune. Usually, a meter of some kind will display this information.

If the string is too low, you'll want to tighten the string by turning it to the left. If the string is too high, you'll want to lower it by turning it to the right. Be sure to listen to the sound of the string as well. Your ear will help you figure out if you are going too far from the in-tune note.

For more help with tuning, be sure to check out The Missing Method YouTube channel. There you will find video tutorials on how to tune your guitar as well as how to keep your guitar in tune. Find it at: https://bit.ly/Missing-Method-YouTube.

ABOUT THE AUTHOR

Over the past 20 years, Christian J. Triola has taught hundreds of students to play guitar and authored over two dozen popular guitar method books. He holds a Master's Degree in Education and a Bachelor's Degree in Music (Jazz Studies), and has played in a variety of bands in addition to his many solo performances.

What is the Missing Method?

We make it easy to learn guitar with books that focus on building one skill at a time. From the basics to chord and note reading mastery, we'll help you build the skills you need to play the music you love.

Find what you've been missing. Visit TheMissingMethod.com.

The Missing Method

Discover what you've been missing.

www.ingramcontent.com/pod-product-compliance
Lightning Source LLC
Chambersburg PA
CBHW081640040426
42449CB00014B/3389